SS, JULY 4, 1776.

thirteen united States of America,

for one people to dissolve the political bands which have connected them with another, and to

Nature's God entitle them, a decent respect to the opinions of mankind requires that they

ruths to be self-evident, that all men are created equal, that they are endowed by their Creator

—— That to secure these rights, Governments are instituted among Men, deriving their just

e of these ends, it is the Right of the People to alter or to abolish it, and to institute new

to them shall seem most likely to effect their Safety and Happiness. Prudence, indeed,

nd accordingly all experience hath shewn, that mankind are more disposed to suffer, while

But when a long train of abuses and usurpations, pursuing invariably the same Object

f such Government, and to provide new Guards for their future security. —— Such has

lter their former Systems of Government. The history of the present King of Great

f an absolute Tyranny over these States. To prove this, let Facts be submitted to a candid

the public good. —————— He has forbidden his Governors to pass Laws of immediate,

d when so suspended, he has utterly neglected to attend to them —————— He has refused to

he right of Representation in the Legislature, a right inestimable to them and formidable

d distant from the depository of their Public Records, for the sole purpose of fatiguing them into

ng with manly firmness his invasions on the rights of the people. —————— He has refused for

ble of Annihilation, have returned to the People at large for their exercise; the State remain-

—— He has endeavoured to prevent the population of these States; for that purpose obstruc-

and raising the conditions of new Appropriations of Lands. —————— He has obstructed the

le has made Judges dependent on his Will alone, for the tenure of their offices, and the amount

arms of Officers to harass our People, and eat out their substance. —————— He has kept among

under the Military independent of and superior to the Civil power? —————— He has combined

giving his Assent to their Acts of pretended Legislation: —— For Quartering large bodies of

ers which they should commit on the Inhabitants of these States: —— For cutting off

depriving us in many cases, of the benefits of Trial by Jury: —— For transporting us beyond

bouring Province, establishing therein an Arbitrary government, and enlarging its Boundaries

ese Colonies: —— For taking away our Charters, abolishing our most valuable Laws, and

d declaring themselves invested with power to legislate for us in all cases whatsoever. —

—— He has plundered our seas, ravaged our coasts, burnt our towns, and destroyed the lives

orks of death, desolation and tyranny, already begun with circumstances of Cruelty & perfidy

Date Due

Thomas Jefferson

Thomas Jefferson *Philosopher of Freedom*

by NEIL R. McMILLEN

RAND McNALLY & COMPANY
CHICAGO · NEW YORK · SAN FRANCISCO

For Caroline and Hunter,
May their generation live up
To Jefferson's dream.

Line drawings, and color illustrations on the front cover
and on pages 26, 27 and 66 by William Jacobson

ENDSHEETS: COURTESY OF THE NATIONAL ARCHIVES AND RECORDS SERVICE

Library of Congress Cataloging in Publication Data

McMillen, Neil R.   1939–
    THOMAS JEFFERSON: philosopher of freedom.

    SUMMARY: A biography of a statesman, lawyer,
architect, inventor, scholar, and president which includes
his roles as husband, father and doting grandfather in
private life.
    1. Jefferson, Thomas, Pres., U.S., 1743–1826—
Juvenile literature. [1. Jefferson, Thomas, Pres., U.S.,
1743–1826.   2. Presidents] I. Title.
E331.M35   1973   973.4'6'0924 [B] [92]   73-12273
ISBN 0-528-82486-4
ISBN 0-528-82487-2 (lib. bdg.)

PRECEDING PAGES:
The Jefferson Memorial, Washington, D.C.
PHOTOGRAPH BY ROLOC

Contents

Introduction

Thomas Jefferson lived in an age when greatness was almost commonplace. Yet he was a giant in his time. Although he was surrounded by some of the most remarkable men in all of human history, he stood then, as he stands today, head and shoulders above all other Founding Fathers. His physical stature, of course, had nothing at all to do with his real greatness. Well over six feet tall, he was a towering figure in a period when a man who even approached six feet was an oddity. But his talents were even more commanding than his height. He may not inspire the awe and reverence of the grave and dignified George Washington or the affection of the folksy, good-humored Benjamin Franklin. He is, however, one of the most fascinating and complex Americans of all time.

As every schoolchild knows, Jefferson was the author of the Declaration of Independence, third president of the United States, and a statesman of extraordinary dedication and ability. His other accomplishments are less well known. Few Americans are aware, for example, that he was one of the most gifted architects of his time. Fewer still think of him as a great scientist and inventor, a scholar, a diplomat, a philosopher and a farmer. He was also a planter and a gadgeteer.

This book is not only about the important things that Thomas Jefferson did; it is also about what Thomas Jefferson was—a warm, vibrant human personality, a considerate son and brother, a loving husband, a devoted father and grandfather, a good neighbor and a faithful friend. Remarkably, he was as good in each of these personal and family roles as he was in his brilliant public life.

Thomas Jefferson had so many sides that he appeals to nearly everyone. Each phase of his life, from childhood and the formation of his magnificent character to his death on July 4, 1836, on the new nation's fiftieth birthday, is a colorful and compelling story.

Let us now turn to the life of this unparalleled champion of the freedom, liberty and dignity of human beings.

Drafting of the Declaration of Independence
by J. L. G. Ferris
Jefferson submits his famous document to the
review of Benjamin Franklin (left) and John Adams.
COURTESY LONGINES SYMPHONETTE SOCIETY

11

This schoolhouse, attended by the
reluctant young Thomas Jefferson, still
stands on the grounds of Tuckahoe Plantation
outside Richmond, Virginia.
COURTESY VIRGINIA STATE LIBRARY

Young Thomas Jefferson

Five-year-old Thomas Jefferson was an uncommonly bright boy. But he did not want to go to school. Even to a future president, the one-room plantation schoolhouse on the Tuckahoe plantation seemed terribly confining. Although his eight-year-old sister, Jane, seemed actually to like the little white "English school," Thomas would have chosen to spend his day elsewhere, running free under the blue Virginia sky. There were trees to climb, fences to scale, and streams in which to wade. Of course, the choice was not really his. And so one unhappy day in 1748, he took his sister's hand and with tears streaming down his ruddy cheeks entered the plantation school to begin one of the most remarkable educations in American history. Later in life, learning and books would become his consuming interests, but just now the plantation school was definitely not the young Jefferson's favorite place.

Indeed Tuckahoe, despite its stately frame and brick mansion and rich, sprawling acreage, was never the boy's favorite corner of the Commonwealth. Born at Shadwell on April 13, 1743, in the wilds of present-day Albemarle County some seventy miles west of Tuckahoe, he was a child of the up-country. Like his father,

Peter, he would always prefer the democratic simplicity of the Piedmont to the aristocratic and cultured plantation society of the Tidewater. Unlike Tuckahoe, his birthplace was a plain and modest farmhouse in a wilderness setting. Here, along the banks of the Rivanna river, in the long, violet shadows of the Blue Ridge mountains, Thomas spent his first years. In 1745, family and business matters required Peter to move his family eastward temporarily to Tuckahoe when Thomas was not quite three. The boy would never think of anyplace but Albemarle County as his home, however. Throughout his long life, his heart belonged to the rolling, red-clay hills on the fringes of Virginia's western settlement.

In his enduring affection for the rugged up-country, Thomas was truly his father's son. Peter, as the son of one of Virginia's oldest families, had inherited some land and even a few slaves. But it was through keen intelligence and hard work, not the advantages of birth, that he acquired a vast plantation, became a justice of the peace and sheriff, and was elected to the colony's legislative body, the House of Burgesses. Although he was a man of property and position, this broad-shouldered giant had the restless spirit of a pioneer. As a young man eager to make his fortune, he bought a one-thousand-acre tract along the Rivanna. Taming the wilderness, he turned forest into farm and built Shadwell with his own hands. Then during Thomas's childhood, while his family still lived at Tuckahoe, Peter turned to the uncharted regions beyond the great Blue Ridge. As a surveyor and map maker, he crossed the hazardous ridges of the Appalachians and forded the swollen mountain streams of western Virginia. He penetrated laurel-choked swamps and virgin forests never seen by white men. Deep in the interior, near the famous Fairfax Stone, he carved the initials P. J. on a giant birch tree. At the age of forty-two, he surveyed the dividing line between North Carolina and Virginia. Today, some two centuries later, the map he drew on this expedition still hangs in the Map Room at the White House in Washington. Unfortunately no other records survive of this, the last and most perilous of Peter's adventures. But his great grandchildren recalled that his assistants, exhausted and hungry, refused to follow him far into the "savage wilderness." But Peter pushed on, threatened by "howling and screeching beasts" by day and sleeping in trees by night. When his provisions were gone he lived on venison. When that could not be found he ate his pack mule. He turned back only when his task was done.

By contrast, Peter's wife, Jane Randolph Jefferson, was a very different kind of person. Born to one of Virginia's proudest and most wealthy families, she could trace her ancestors back to early England and Scotland. A gentle, delicate woman not well suited for life on the frontier, she was, nonetheless, a devoted and loving wife. She brought cheer, humor, and children in great numbers into the life of her quiet and serious-minded husband. She bore him six daughters and four sons.

In appearance and personality, the young future president exhibited many of Jane Randolph Jefferson's characteristics. Although tall and plain featured like his father, Thomas was never as strongly built as Peter. His thin frame, his amiable·and affectionate disposition, his ready laughter and easy charm, clearly marked him as Jane Randolph's son. His character, however, bore the unmistakable stamp of Peter Jefferson. As father and son their years together were few. At the age of nine Thomas went away to boarding school, and soon after his fourteenth birthday Peter died. But however brief, this relationship had a lasting impact on the son. From his father he learned to judge people by their merits and not by their family trees. Peter had known and understood the raw, unlettered men of the frontier; Thomas grew up with a natural respect for the common man. The boy also shared the elder Jefferson's respect for nature and his fascination for the unspoiled wilderness west of the Blue Ridge. Neither of them could have suspected then that one day Thomas, as president of the United States, would

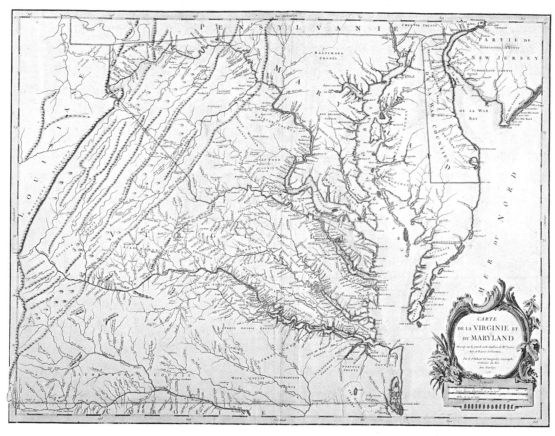

A 1755 French version of the Maryland-Virginia
area mapped by Peter Jefferson (Thomas Jefferson's father)
and his associate, Joshua Fry. It now hangs
on the east wall of the White House Map Room.

order the exploration and purchase of that vast western region. But who could doubt that the fires of the boy's westering imagination were kindled by the tales his explorer-map maker father told?

It seems likely, too, that Thomas's life-long interest in the Indians can be traced to Peter's influence. There were no Indian inhabitants nearby when Shadwell was built, but the leaders of these original Virginians occasionally passed through their ancestral lands enroute to the colonial capital in Williamsburg. Peter befriended them and they were always welcome guests at Shadwell. Years later, as governor and president, Thomas would receive many Indian visitors. He would address them as "Father" and smoke their peace pipes. Perhaps he told them of the times so many years before when others of their tribes paused to rest at his boyhood home on the Rivanna river.

Peter Jefferson had little formal education, and all of his life regretted this. He could read and write, and he even owned a small library of some forty volumes on geography, astronomy, English literature and history. Like many fathers, then and now, he wanted more for his son. When he died, in 1757, he left his fourteen-year-old son an established position in Virginia society and the income to enjoy it. The boy's inheritance included slaves and a large estate, his father's books and bookcase, his cherry wood desk and his many surveying instruments. This was a handsome legacy by any measure. But the things themselves meant less to Thomas than his memories of life with this rugged but soft-spoken giant of the wilderness country. Most of all he remembered Peter's last wish. On his deathbed the elder Jefferson directed his son and heir to use his inheritance to obtain the education that he had been denied. Later in life Thomas would say that his father left him much—but nothing half so important as the will to learn.

Perhaps because he spent most of his young life away at school, he was also an unusually loving son and brother. He helped his mother when he could. He was devoted to his sisters, most of all to Jane, who encouraged his studies and shared his love of nature and music. Especially he delighted in Anna Scott and Randolph, the playful twins who were born when he was away at the Reverend Mr. Douglas's school. In later years these Jefferson children would cherish warm memories of their serious brother. They remembered him as a boy who loved to be out of doors. They remembered the long hours he spent in the rolling Piedmont countryside observing and recording the growth of wild flowers and the habits of woodland creatures. And when he became president, his grandchildren took special delight in hearing tales of their famous grandfather's childhood pastimes and adventures.

After his father's death, the earnest young scholar moved to the Reverend James Maury's log schoolhouse only twelve miles from his home. He was still too far from Shadwell to live with his family, but at least now he could come home weekends on horseback. Under the guidance of his new teacher, Jefferson continued his study of the ancient languages of classical Greece and Rome. He read English literature and the Bible. He learned some geography, history and mathematics. Within two years he finished his preparation and, although he was only sixteen, his schoolmaster announced that he was now ready for college.

In 1760, the year George III became king of England, Jefferson left the hills of Albemarle for Williamsburg to enter the College of William and Mary. In many respects it was a strange choice for the future champion of religious liberty. Although its president was a widely known drunkard, the college, like most other colleges of its day, was a church-affiliated institution founded to train "ministers of the Gospel." Moreover, it was not well regarded by the colony's well-to-do, who considered it more a school of "manners and Morals" than a place of higher learning. Such famous Virginians as John Taylor of Caroline, John Marshall and James Monroe would later follow Jefferson to William and Mary, but most young men of the time sought their education in England or at the better-known schools of the New England colonies. The independent-minded young Mr. Jefferson sought his in the provincial capital of Virginia, where he could still look after his mother and watch over his estate.

Although it was a village of only 1,500 people when he arrived, Williamsburg was the center of Virginia politics, society and culture. It was smaller than

either Norfolk or Petersburg, the colony's other important cities. It had three hundred houses, however, a newspaper office, a book shop and a quaint "L"-shaped tavern named after Sir Walter Raleigh. Its main thoroughfare, the Duke of Gloucester Street, was fully one hundred feet wide, and it stretched nearly a mile from the front steps of the college to the great columns of the Capitol building. Walking for the first time along this "noble great street," the dazzled newcomer took in the strange sights and sounds of a city. There was a seemingly endless procession of coaches churning the oyster shell-surfaced street into a fine white powder. There was the grassy openness of the Palace Green, and a large empty space called the Exchange where on market days planters sold barrels of tobacco to British merchants and bought black slaves from Africa. There were crowded little shops and the Coffee House, a great brick church, a theater and race track. He saw it all, including the Public Gaol (jail), where prisoners were kept, and the gallows, where the worst of them were hanged. It was the most exciting place he had ever been.

The student himself was a curious sight. Lean and strong, already more than six feet tall and still growing, this loose-jointed, angular seventeen-year-old seemed to be developing right out of his clothes. Neither handsome nor graceful, his tousled light red hair and searching hazel eyes, ruddy cheeks and freckled face made him look every inch the country lad he was. Williamsburg would soon learn, however, that his rustic appearance was deceiving.

His teachers recognized almost immediately that "Long Tom" Jefferson was well prepared for the college's difficult program of study in the "systems of logick, physicks, ethicks and mathematicks." Working often as many as fifteen hours each day, he usually studied long past midnight and always rose at dawn. Even on vacation he spent most of his hours either reading or searching for sheet music for his violin and books for his growing library.

Yet he was much more than a bookworm. He spent many evenings at dinner, chamber music and conversation at the Governor's Palace, in the company of Governor Francis Fauquier, Professor William Small and Judge George Wythe. He found, he later said, "much instruction," and also an opportunity to relax with older gentlemen who knew about life as well as books. In other free moments he went to the theater, joined a frivolous social club, took music lessons and jogged and swam with fellow students. He was always a rather private person, but he enjoyed good company and made friends easily. He often shared a toast with the merry young gentlemen of Williamsburg at the Apollo Room in the city's famous Raleigh Tavern. Occasionally he even played a hand of cards and placed a bet on a favorite horse. But he was neither a gambler nor a ladies' man. And he was usually so unconcerned about his appearance that his friends urged him to dress more carefully in order to win favor with the opposite sex. Apparently he followed this advice. For one spring, about the time he finished college, he fell madly in love with the beautiful and popular sixteen-year-old Rebecca Burwell.

It was only temporary, however. Twice during a year-long courtship he stumbled awkwardly through well-rehearsed efforts to express his love. Before he could speak his heart clearly, she agreed to marry one of his friends. He was heartbroken, he thought. But he agreed to serve as best man at the wedding. The whole experience taught him, he wrote in his notebook, that a woman could only steal a man's freedom. He would think of marriage again, he said, only after he was "old and weary of the world."

There were, of course, other things to interest him. Already a wealthy land owner, he could have retired to Shadwell to lead the free and easy life of a tobacco planter. He wanted to be neither a soldier nor a merchant. He could have studied medicine to become a physician, or theology to become a minister. Both professions were respectable and quite suitable for a man of his social class. Yet he found law more attractive. It would challenge his mind and make him useful to society. It would provide an ample income and still permit him time to manage his estate. Thus, he chose to become a lawyer.

In his day there were no regularly organized law schools and no formal requirements for admission to that profession. By common practice a student studied law at his own pace under the direction of an established lawyer. Some, like the brilliant and fiery orator Patrick Henry, flew through a hasty program of self-study in only six months. But Jefferson, who was always critical of Henry's shallow legal knowledge, pursued a long and difficult program. He read the complex legal works of Sir Edward Coke. "Old Coke," as he called him, was a "dull scoundrel," but a man to be admired as a champion of English rights and liberties. He studied such everyday legal matters as wills and contracts, theft and trespassing. He kept careful notes in his "commonplace books" on the important cases he wanted to remember. To relax and "learn the full powers of the English language," he read Shakespeare's plays. In 1767, after five years of the most painstaking study, the twenty-four-year-old Virginian began his legal career. He would never stop learning. But his formal education was now behind him. He was ready at last, he declared, for the "business of life."

The business of Jefferson's life, however, was not the practice of law. Although he continued in that occupation for seven years, he was never very fond of it. His true calling was public service. His occupation was leadership. From his entry into the colonial legislature in 1769 to his retirement from the White House in 1809, he gave forty years of devoted service to his country. In turn, he was a member of the House of Burgesses, the Continental Congress, and the Virginia House of Delegates. He was governor, minister to France, secretary of state, vice president and president. He wrote the Declaration of Independence and the Virginia Statute of Religious Freedom. To his lasting regret he was on government service in Europe when the Constitution was written. Jefferson's "business," in short, was to fix the course of American democracy. He did not know it that glad day in 1767 when he was admitted to the bar, but the name of this up-country lawyer would live in history as the philosopher of freedom.

The Apprentice Statesman

It was mid-January, 1772, and Virginia was hit by one of the worst blizzards in memory. In the gathering shadows of the evening the snow, already three feet deep, fell in great white flakes that clung to the carriage top and the shaggy winter coats of Jefferson's horses. On the exposed front seat of the four-wheeled phaeton sat Jupiter, the Negro coachman, shivering wearily in the cold. Impatiently, he urged the tired animals on through the drifts. He was hungry and he longed for the cozy warmth of his master's slave quarters not far ahead. From behind him, inside the black leather folds of the carriage top, came laughter and singing. It was not much warmer there, but to young lovers even the cold of a winter's night could be forgotten in the warmth of a long embrace.

Thomas Jefferson was taking his new wife home through the blinding snow to the little mountain he called Monticello. Martha Wayles Skelton, his bride, was a small, auburn-haired, twenty-three-year-old beauty whose large, sad hazel eyes reflected the tragedies of her earlier life. Death had claimed her first husband and their son, yet she rarely dwelt on the sorrows of the past. She loved Jefferson dearly, and she shared his passion for music. In fact, he won her, people said, around the harpsichord in her father's parlor, where each played and sang into the other's heart.

Now after a leisurely wedding trip from The Forest, her family's estate on the James river, they stopped briefly in the valley below Monticello to exchange their carriage for horseback. Then, on through the ghostly winter night they rode, up a

21

Honeymoon Cottage was the first building
completed by Jefferson, and it was here that he lived
with Martha until the main mansion was
completed. The small domed structure covers
a well. Right, the interior of Honeymoon Cottage,
to which he brought his bride on a snowy
January night in 1772.

winding trail eight miles to Honeymoon Lodge, a one-room brick cottage on the mountaintop. For the moment, the Lodge was Monticello's main structure. It would serve as Martha's kitchen and Thomas's study, their parlor and their bed-room. Later, as Monticello's handsome mansion neared completion, Honeymoon Lodge would look even smaller. But there, in happy isolation, they remained the rest of the winter. In February, the House of Burgesses met without Jefferson. Not until the mountainside turned green did he leave Martha's side to attend to affairs in the colonial capital.

Now thirty years old, Jefferson had been a member of the House of Burgesses for four years. It was interesting, often exciting, work. Yet it demanded compara-tively little of his time. Between sessions in Williamsburg he practiced law, super-vised the construction of Monticello, and tended to the endless round of activity on his farms. But whatever the season and whatever his immediate concern, his mind was never very far from politics and the approaching struggle with England. Although the war for American independence was still three eventful years away, a spirit of rebellion was already sweeping across the colonies.

Basically, the quarrel with the mother country centered on the issue of colonial self-rule. The thirteen colonies, the Americans claimed, should govern themselves through their own legislatures without interference from the British Parliament. It was not their intention at this point to be disloyal to their king. But because no colonists sat in Parliament, it was not proper for Parliament to make laws for the colonies.

Although reasonable enough from the colonists' point of view, this argument was not accepted by British officials. Parliamentary authority, the English govern-ment countered, extended to all the king's subjects—whether they lived in Lon-don, England, or Williamsburg, Virginia.

The question of home rule was almost as old as the colonial governments themselves. But it was never a very serious question until about the time that Jefferson began his study of law. Then, in 1764, following a series of long and costly wars with France and her Indian allies, Great Britain tried to tax her New World subjects to raise money for her empty treasury. The Americans benefited from these wars, the English rulers reasoned, so it was only fair that they help pay for them. These new taxes were actually not very high when compared to those already paid by English landowners. But the colonists believed that there was an important principle, as well as money, at stake here. Not only was taxation with-out representation unfair, but Parliament's attempt to meddle in American affairs was also a serious threat to self-government.

From his earliest days in Williamsburg, Jefferson watched this controversy un-fold. He was present when Patrick Henry boldly denounced the Stamp Act, and he heartily approved when colonists resisted British efforts to collect the Townshend duties (taxes) on all glass, paint, lead, paper and tea sold in the New World. Upon his election to the House of Burgesses, he immediately became involved. Unlike his emotional friend, Patrick Henry, one of the earliest Americans to favor independence, Jefferson would never be counted among the "hot heads," but he was always identified with the more impatient young patriots of the up-country who favored vigorous opposition to Parliamentary rule.

The new Burgess did not care for the role of a public speaker, and therefore said little before the entire body of the House. But in small committees, where most of the work of the colonial legislature was accomplished, he won wide respect as a thoughtful and persuasive defender of colonial rights. Whenever there was need for a formal written statement, a resolution, or a law, he was called upon to write it. Already known locally for his broad learning and his clear and direct literary style, he was rapidly emerging as one of the New World's most able critics of British colonial policy. While he would win his greatest fame as the author of the Declaration of Independence, early recognition came in 1774 after the appearance of his *Summary View of the Rights of British America*. In this justly famous essay, the apprentice statesman dismissed Parliamentary authority altogether. The colonies' only tie with England, he argued, was their common devotion to the crown. Although others, including wise old Benjamin Franklin, had said as much before, no one had ever presented the argument more boldly and with such dignity and force. Almost overnight, Jefferson found himself in the center of important colonial affairs.

In his personal life, however, there was often tragedy. In May, 1773, workmen prepared a small cemetery beneath a great oak on the side of Jefferson's mountain. Years before, in his boyhood, Thomas and his closest friend, Dabney Carr, had sprawled under that very tree to read and dream and while away their summer afternoons. They were classmates then at the Reverend James Maury's log schoolhouse and later at the College of William and Mary. In time, Dabney married Thomas's sister, Martha, practiced law, and joined his brother-in-law in the House of Burgesses. But that spring he died suddenly of bilious fever, leaving behind six children. In fulfillment of a childhood promise, Jefferson buried Dabney in the shade of their favorite oak. He now had two Marthas (his wife and his sister), three nephews, and three nieces to care for. Obviously there was not room in tiny Honeymoon Lodge for the seven Carrs, who had their own home nearby. But once the main house on Monticello was finished, the Jeffersons brought them all into their new home.

Not long after Dabney's death, workmen dug other graves beneath the sacred oak. The Jeffersons' first child, Patsy, was born in the autumn of 1772. Although

sickly and often near death during her first six months, this baby lived to become a strong and healthy child. The next year, however, a second daughter died when only a few months old. About the same time Martha's father, John Wayles, and Thomas's sister, Elizabeth, both died. Already the little cemetery carried a sad and heavy burden.

Fortunately all was not death and sorrow at Monticello. Jefferson's beloved Martha still had good health, and Patsy was a fine, fat, laughing baby. Work at Monticello was progressing, however slowly, and Jefferson had even found time to plant fruit trees and a vegetable garden which included beans, onions, garlic and endive on the sunny south slope. He had no pressing debts. His income was more than comfortable. To make things seem absolutely perfect, his prize blooded mare, Young Fearnought, delivered a bright-eyed, wobbly-legged colt. He called the young stallion Caractacus. It would be years before Patsy could pronounce the name, but she soon considered this wonderful creature her very own. For the moment, at least, Jefferson believed that he would be content to spend the rest of his life in this pleasant little world on the mountaintop.

The next year, however, the colonial argument with England became a war. On April 19, 1775, patriot Minutemen exchanged gunfire with Redcoats at Lexington and Concord, Massachusetts. Two months later, at Breed's Hill (not Bunker Hill)

OVERLEAF: Mrs. Clementina Rind was the public printer in Williamsburg, Virginia at the time that Thomas Jefferson wrote his *Summary View of the Rights of British America,* which he brought to her to be set in type. George Washington, among others, bought his copy from Mrs. Rind for three shillings and ninepence.

American and British soldiers fought the first and bloodiest battle of the American Revolutionary War. Although few suspected it then, eight years of hard fighting lay ahead.

In June, Jefferson left Monticello by carriage for Philadelphia, ten long days and 325 difficult miles away. He had been called to join sixty-four other patriot leaders from every colony but distant Georgia in the white-paneled chamber of Pennsylvania's colonial State House. Later called Independence Hall, this handsome red brick structure was the seat of the second Continental Congress, already in session.

Although he cared little for cities, Jefferson, the country gentleman, found Philadelphia, with its paved and lighted streets and its 34,000 inhabitants, to be a place of interest. Always a busy city, it seemed especially so now. Irregular troops called Quaker Blues and Philadelphia Associaters were drilling and practicing in nearly every open space. Small wonder, then, that the city looked like an army camp. News of the British victory at Breed's Hill had just arrived. Congress had named the forty-three-year-old Colonel George Washington commander in chief of a ragtag patriot army of 14,000 troops. As Jefferson well understood, the Virginia military leader's task was no easy one. His army was an army in name only. It had few uniforms, little training, and almost no money or supplies. Still, the gallant Washington promised to use "every power I possess . . . for the support of this glorious Cause."

No one who knew Washington doubted his considerable powers. Certainly all but the British and their American friends, the Tories, could agree that the cause was glorious. But what exactly was it? The Americans were fighting a war, but for what purpose? Were they seeking independence from England? Or were they simply fighting for their rights as Englishmen? Was George III their king? Or was he merely the king of the enemy soldiers they were now fighting?

As Jefferson quickly learned, the distinguished men gathered at the State House could not agree upon the answers to these questions. They sent Washington off to Boston to confront the British. They organized an army and a navy, and even sent diplomats to Europe and an armed force to Canada. They could, in short, support the war effort. But they could not agree upon the war aim. Some, such as John Adams and Samuel Adams of Massachusetts, believed that the "glorious Cause" was independence. Although they hardly dared say so yet, the Adamses believed that the colonies must now separate entirely from England. Others, like cautious, conservative John Dickinson of Pennsylvania, hoped that peace and harmony could soon be restored and the colonies and their mother country reconciled. Thomas Jefferson and most of the other members of Congress were somewhere in between. They were ready to fight for self-government, but not to break openly with Great Britain. They still hoped that colonial rights could be protected within the framework of English government.

Throughout the long, hot Pennsylvania summer and well into the winter the debate in the State House continued. When Jefferson went home to Martha in December, 1775, the questions surrounding the "glorious Cause" were still unanswered. When he returned to Philadelphia in May, 1776, the period of uncertainty was nearly over. The five months from December to May had been a time of decision for America. During the winter and early spring of 1776 the people made up their minds. King George had declared them in a "state of rebellion" and ordered all "traitors" brought to justice. Even worse, he now used the hated Hessians, the Indians and runaway slaves in his war against them. Reluctantly, they agreed with Thomas Paine, author of *Common Sense,* that it was foolish to remain loyal to a distant king who treated them so badly. Paine's peppery little book did not cause their feelings of ill will toward England's "crowned ruffian." But it helped the Americans to see that the road to independence was the only road still open to them.

Back in Philadelphia on June 7, Jefferson listened attentively when Richard Henry Lee, his friend and fellow Virginian, rose in the State House to resolve "that these United Colonies are, and of right ought to be, free and independent states." Then, as Congress considered this resolution, he met with Benjamin Franklin and John Adams to prepare a formal declaration of American independence. The aged Franklin was suffering from gout. His big toe was painfully sore, he said, and his younger associates, Adams and Jefferson, should prepare the first draft. But Adams thought otherwise. He was, he admitted with some embarrassment, "obnoxious, suspected, and unpopular." Jefferson was not. Besides, the Virginia statesman could write "ten times better" than Adams. And so the task was Jefferson's. Promising to "do as well as I can," he went to work.

He worked day and night for more than two weeks. When he was finished it was clear that he had done well indeed. Adams and Franklin suggested only minor changes. Congress insisted on a few of its own. Some of these alterations the thin-skinned author thought unnecessary; others offended him greatly. But he agreed that the finished document must be one they could all accept. And accept it they did, late in the evening of July 4, 1776.

By unanimous declaration, the thirteen American states proclaimed it "self-evident, that all men are created equal; that they are endowed by their Creator with certain unalienable rights; that among these, are life, liberty, and the pursuit of happiness." The sole purpose of any government, Congress declared, was to protect the rights of those it governed and when it did not "it is the right of the people to alter or to abolish it, and to institute a new government."

These noble words were Jefferson's, but the ideas, he freely admitted, were not his alone. The equality of all men before God and nature! The right of people to rule themselves! The right to make and unmake government as the need arose! These were the ideas of the great English philosopher John Locke. They were the ideas of the Enlightenment, of the humane and liberal eighteenth-century thinkers of both sides of the Atlantic who dared to believe that freedom was man's birthright. They were original to neither the Virginia statesman nor the American people. But Jefferson reshaped them into a foundation for liberty upon which the people would build a free and independent state.

30

Presentation of the Declaration of Independence
by John Trumbull

When the Declaration was announced on July 8, jubilant Philadelphians rang bells and pulled the royal coat of arms from the State House. In New York, patriots melted a statue of George III into bullets, and joyous Bostonians burned a straw figure they called the king. Not everybody, however, was pleased at the news. Tories, or loyalists, as they preferred to be known, did not favor independence. Nor did they believe that the patriot cause was in any way glorious. Numbering well into the thousands, many Tories had already left this land of rebellion. Others now hastily departed, or kept their unpopular opinions to themselves for fear of being tarred and feathered.

The author himself was in no mood for celebration. The Declaration, he knew, was only a beginning. To separate from England was not enough. Now a new government must be formed. He lingered impatiently in Philadelphia until September, and then rode off to help build a new Virginia.

Making the trip home in only six days, he paused at Monticello just long enough to put his neglected personal affairs in order, and gather up Martha and Patsy. October found the three of them living in Williamsburg. They were hardly settled, however, when word came that Jefferson had been appointed by Congress to help Benjamin Franklin negotiate a treaty of friendship with France. It was an honor and a temptation. He had never been abroad before, and he wanted especially to visit Paris. But after three days of careful thought he respectfully refused. Martha was recovering slowly from a summer-long illness and could not make the ocean voyage. For the remainder of her life he would never stray far from her side again. France would have to wait.

Next to Martha's frail health, his one great concern for the next three years was his work in the Virginia House of Delegates. While he was away at Congress, the Commonwealth had adopted a new constitution that was not at all to his liking. The new charter did not represent the high ideals of the Declaration of Independence. It contained too many holdovers from the Commonwealth's royal past. The proud, rich aristocrats who ruled Virginia before the Revolution continued to rule over the common people. The only real difference was that they now ruled in their own names instead of the king's.

Actually, Jefferson had no quarrel with either aristocrats or aristocracy. How could he? A brilliant, well-educated and cultured gentleman of property, he had little in common with the ignorant masses. Yet he believed that the best government was the government led by those who were best qualified to lead. The abilities and virtues required for leadership had nothing at all to do with riches or birth, and could be found in citizens from every class and station of life. The major flaw in the Virginia constitution, then, was that it formed a government based on privilege, not talent. His task was to correct that flaw.

Jefferson helped prepare 126 laws for the new state. All were important, but most concerned such routine matters as the arrest of horse thieves and the prevention of disease among cattle. But others sought to correct abuses, to right wrongs, and to expand liberties. In a very real sense, Jefferson's work in the House of Delegates was based on his belief that there was more to the Revolution than independence. Consistently, he tried to apply the broad and lofty ideas of his Declaration of Independence to the practical, everyday realities of life in a free society.

Of all his proposals, he regarded his Bill for Religious Freedom as the most important. A kind of declaration of spiritual independence, this law freed Virginians to worship, or not worship, as they chose. Next in importance, he thought, was his Bill for the More General Diffusion of Knowledge. Believing that ignorance was the enemy of democracy, he proposed a system of free education for all citizens. His elaborate plan for public education was rejected, but eventually Virginia created a free public school system. He also worked to end cruel and inhumane punishment for minor crimes, and to promote a wider distribution of land ownership and voting privileges. He helped to originate a line of thought that ultimately ended the slave trade, but he failed to win support for his plan for the gradual freeing of the slaves.

The revision of state laws occupied Jefferson's attention until June, 1779, when he succeeded Patrick Henry as governor. An appointive, rather than an elective office, the governorship was thrust upon him by the Virginia legislature. He accepted it as the unpleasant but necessary duty it was.

As a war governor, his most pressing duties concerned the struggle with England. General Washington was always in need of more soldiers, more supplies and more money for weapons and payrolls. The eleven battalions Virginia sent to the Continental army required an unending stream of new recruits to replace the dead and wounded. It was the governor's job to find these replacements, as well as to supply the army with flour, corn, hay and rum.

In meeting the needs of the Continental army, however, the governor found that Virginia itself could not be adequately defended. In 1781, British troops under the turncoat General Benedict Arnold and Lord Charles Cornwallis drove the legislature and governor from the new capital in Richmond into temporary quarters in Charlottesville, near Monticello. But even here they were nearly captured by English cavalry.

Fortunately by this time, however, both Jefferson's term of office and the war were nearly over. In October, 1781, Washington defeated Cornwallis at Yorktown in the last major battle of the Revolution.

With the war and his responsibilities now behind him, Jefferson informed an acquaintance that "I have . . . retired to my farm, my family and books from which I think nothing will ever more separate me." Offered appointments as peace negotiator in Paris and delegate to Congress, he refused them both. After thirteen years of continuous public service his personal affairs required his full attention. His family was larger now. In 1777, an unnamed son had died soon after birth, but the following year Polly, a strong and healthy girl, arrived. In addition there were, of course, Patsy, now six, and the six Carr children. This happy houseful was his "sacred charge." He taught the older ones their lessons, lavished affection on them all, and retreated periodically from their noise to work on his book, *Notes on the State of Virginia.* Full of his observations on nature, politics, science and philosophy, this remarkable volume would soon win the praise of learned men on both sides of the Atlantic.

A sorrowful entry in an account book for September 6, 1782 noted: "My dear wife died this day at 11:45 A.M." Martha's death after a prolonged illness plunged Jefferson into profound grief. As Patsy later recalled: "He kept [to] his room three weeks.... He walked almost night and day, only lying down occasionally.... When at last he left his room, he rode out, and from that time he was incessantly on horseback, rambling about the mountain . . . [and] through the woods."

Without Martha, Jefferson was lost and heartbroken, and his quiet mountain refuge was not the same to him. His friends were worried about him and they tried to persuade him to return to public life. The Virginia House of Delegates returned him to Congress in 1783 and he occupied himself totally with the nation's business. This second phase of his congressional career was brief, but remarkably productive. He served on virtually every major committee, helped shape government land policy for the unsettled west, and assisted in the passage of a treaty ending the American Revolutionary War. He also introduced the decimal money system, which substituted easily-counted dollars, dimes and pennies for the more awkward English pounds, shillings and pence. Unfortunately, Congress did not adopt his proposal for an equally logical system of weights and measures.

In July, 1784, Congress sent him to Europe to join his old friends Franklin and Adams in negotiating foreign trade agreements. In 1785, when Franklin retired, Jefferson became America's chief diplomat in France.

Jefferson found Paris enjoyable in many ways. He renewed his friendship with the Marquis de Lafayette, who had fought with the Americans in the War. Jefferson made many new friends in Paris, one of whom was the beautiful Maria Cosway, with whom he spent many a pleasant afternoon.

Patsy and Polly, who spent some of these years at a convent school not far from their father's work, found Europe exciting and educational. Yet they longed for the more familiar world across the Atlantic. After five years abroad, they were not at all unhappy when Jefferson said in 1789 that he was taking them and their shepherd dog, Bergere, back to Monticello. The girls would remain at home with friends and family. Their father, after putting his estate in order, would return to his post in France.

Once back on Virginia soil, however, these plans changed. President Washington announced that Jefferson had been appointed as the nation's first secretary of state. Although he was reluctant and did not reach a final decision for several months, he could hardly refuse such an honor.

Clearly there was excitement in the air for them all. Jefferson would have an active role in leading a new nation. Patsy, now seventeen, would soon wed a handsome young Virginian she had met in Paris. Little Polly could introduce her shepherd dog to the sunny meadows and cool woodlands of Albemarle County. And Bergere? She was expecting a litter of puppies!

Power and Glory: The Politics of Freedom

Jefferson was not eager for the position of national leadership that Washington offered. The new secretary of state, whoever he was, would need exceptional talents. He must look after the new nation's affairs with foreign countries, take the census, grant patents, copyrights and pardons, supervise the enforcement of laws and tend to relations between the national government and the states and territories. Only a wizard, Jefferson believed, could handle such a job. Wizardry was not one of his gifts, and he had little taste for the public criticism that failure in this new assignment would surely bring.

Nor was he ready to give up Paris. After so many years in Europe's most beautiful and civilized city, New York had few attractions for him. The drab temporary capital of the United States, he believed, had neither a spring nor a fall, and its winter was fully ten months long. Even its two summer months had some disagreeably cold days.

If a wintry April in New York was a far cry from an April in Paris, it was even farther from an April in Albemarle County. By April, the spring planting at Monticello was already well under way. For too many springs Jefferson had left his farms in the care of others. If he could not return to the ministry in France, he would be quite content to retire to his mountaintop.

All of these thoughts ran through his head as he read and reread Washington's letter of appointment. In the end, however, he could not refuse. He would have to

President George Washington and his cabinet; (from left) Henry Knox, secretary of war; Alexander Hamilton, secretary of the treasury; Thomas Jefferson, secretary of state; Edmund Randolph, attorney general.

miss yet another Monticello April. Leaving Polly in the motherly care of a favorite aunt and Patsy in the arms of Thomas Mann Randolph, her new husband, in March, 1790, he made haste to New York.

The government he now served as secretary of state was considerably changed from the government he knew in the Continental Congress. The Confederation government, organized under the Articles of Confederation in 1777, had been replaced by a government organized under the Constitution of 1787. The Confederation was probably the best government that could have been formed during the Revolution. But it proved inadequate to meet the needs of a growing nation. To form a "more perfect union," the Founding Fathers returned to the State House in Philadelphia during the summer of 1787. There, under the wise leadership of Jefferson's young friend James Madison, they wrote the Constitution.

Jefferson himself was abroad when this new plan of government was written, but Madison kept him well informed. More than most men, Jefferson feared tyranny. He favored a stronger union than the Confederation provided. But he feared that the Constitution gave too much authority to the national government. These early doubts were overcome, however, when the first ten amendments (the Bill of Rights) were added to protect such basic human rights and liberties as freedom of speech, press and religion. With these changes, he believed, the American Constitution was "the wisest ever yet presented to men."

When he arrived in New York in the early spring of 1790 to join this new government, the other chief officers of the United States were already at work. The year before, Washington and Adams had been chosen president and vice president, and an attorney general and the secretaries of war and the treasury had been appointed. Jefferson had no reason to assume that he could not work harmoniously with this distinguished group of statesmen.

Very soon, however, it was clear that Alexander Hamilton, the young New Yorker who was secretary of the treasury, was not as agreeable as he first appeared. The two men differed in almost every way. Hamilton was as short as Jefferson was tall. Jefferson was rather plain looking and careless of fashion; Hamilton was a handsome dandy. Hamilton could be gracious. But he was quick to anger and often rude.

Obviously, the secretary of state differed greatly in appearance and temperament from the secretary of the treasury. On issues of public policy and public service he differed even more. Hamilton loved power and aggressively sought positions of influence. Jefferson preferred private to public life. Like Washington he did not seek high office; he reluctantly accepted it as a duty, not a pleasure.

Moreover, Jefferson, the champion of human rights, feared Hamilton's aristocratic political ideas. It was Hamilton's desire, he soon realized, to undermine the Declaration of Independence and undo the Revolution by returning to hereditary privilege. The little New Yorker greatly admired the British system of rule by royalty and aristocrats. He distrusted common people and believed that the "better people," "the rich and well born," were the only class fit to govern.

The Virginian could not have disagreed more. Indeed, he spent most of his three years in Washington's administration opposing Hamilton's financial programs. "Every day in the Cabinet," he wrote a friend, "we battled like two fighting cocks." He reluctantly agreed to the secretary of the treasury's measures for paying American debts and establishing sound credit. But he objected to Hamilton's plans for a national bank and for encouraging shipping and manufacturing. These Hamiltonian or Federalist programs violated Jefferson's "strict construction" theories. Jefferson believed that the government could exercise only those powers specifically *granted* by the Constitution. Hamilton and the Federalists, on the other hand, argued for a "loose" interpretation of governmental authority. The government, they declared, could do anything not specifically *forbidden* by the Constitution. Consequently, Federalist programs generally favored the national government at the expense of the states, the industrial North at the expense of the agricultural South, and merchants and bankers at the expense of working people and farmers. The Federalists also sought closer ties with England, while Jefferson and his followers, the Democratic-Republicans (then called Republicans and later known as Democrats) preferred to continue a close relationship with France.

Thus, in time, the differing views of Jefferson and Hamilton became the basis for political parties. President Washington opposed political strife and valued Jefferson's advice. But he favored Federalist policies and usually agreed with Hamilton's programs. He tried to keep both of these bitter rivals in his cabinet; but Jefferson soon wearied of the "hated occupation of politics." In late 1793, he resigned to reenter "the society of my neighbors and my books, in the wholesome occupations of my farms and my affairs."

In retirement, however, Jefferson did not put the "hated occupation" altogether behind him. Even at Monticello he was clearly the leading critic of Federalism, and in 1796 he became the Democratic-Republican candidate for the presidency. He did not seek the office, and he did not campaign for it. But his party boasted that he was a "steadfast friend to the rights of the people," while his Federalist opponent, John Adams, was the "champion of rank, titles, and hereditary distinctions."

Adams won the election, and under the laws of the day, Jefferson became vice president. "The second office," he said philosophically, "is honorable and easy, the first is but splendid misery."

In fact, Vice President Jefferson found little to do in the Adams administration except keep order in the Senate. Adams was no friend of Hamilton and he agreed

with Washington that political bickering served no useful purpose. But he was a Federalist, nevertheless. Once again Jefferson found himself in the uncomfortable position of opposing an old friend.

Actually, Adams was never as extreme as some members of his party, and he resisted the demands of the High Federalists, the Hamiltonians, to declare war on France. But his policies were consistently unpopular with Jefferson and his followers, and during his administration unwise measures were passed to crush all political opposition. Called the Alien and Sedition Acts, these offensive laws were denounced by Jefferson and Madison in the Virginia and Kentucky Resolutions as an unconstitutional attack on individual liberty.

In this atmosphere of "politics and party hatreds" even the best friendships could not survive. As fellow Revolutionaries and members of the old Continental Congress, Adams and Jefferson were good friends. But as president and vice president they became bitter political foes. In 1800, they both sought the office of the presidency. It was no credit to either of them that the campaign of that year was one of the dirtiest in American history.

After the election, it was clear that Adams, the Federalist candidate, had lost —but the balloting in the electoral college brought the first and only tie in American history. A flaw in the election process left Jefferson and his vice presidential running mate, Aaron Burr, with the same number of votes. A more honorable man than Burr would have stepped aside. But Burr, whatever else he was, was not a man of honor. The matter was finally resolved in the House of Representatives, where, oddly enough, Alexander Hamilton used his influence to secure Burr's defeat and Jefferson's victory. The twelfth amendment to the Constitution was soon ratified to prevent another such deadlock.

The election of Jefferson ended twelve years of Federalist rule. According to his party, the Democratic-Republicans, it brought the "Revolution of 1800." The new president himself believed that his victory "was as real a revolution in the principles of government as that of 1776 was in its form." The election, he believed, saved the country from Federalist tyranny and perhaps even monarchy. Of course, Jefferson exaggerated, as politicians usually do, when he spoke of the dangers posed by his political foes. But clearly he brought to the new capital city of Washington a more democratic approach to national leadership than had been practiced previously. President Adams had encouraged the use of such formal titles as "His Excellency" and "Her Ladyship" for high public officials and their wives. There was even an effort to call President Washington "His Highness, the President of the United States, and Protector of their Liberties." Jefferson, who was never very good at bowing and scraping, viewed all such royal leftovers as Federalist foolishness. "Mr. President," he thought, was a more fitting title for the elected leader of a free people.

The easy informality of his style of leadership was apparent from his first day as president. On the day of his inauguration the fifty-seven-year-old statesman slipped quietly from his boarding house and walked almost unnoticed up New Jersey Avenue, across the square, and into the Capitol to take the oath of office. There was no great parade. Certainly there was no fancy coach with elegant trappings.

From that day on, when he went about the city he usually rode Wildair, his handsome bay horse. Many of the city's more snobbish inhabitants believed it unbecoming for the head of state to travel so informally. But Jefferson cared little for snobbery. He was an up-country Virginian, and he preferred to travel on horseback. Moreover, these quiet rides gave him an opportunity to meet the citizens. On one such occasion he paused to talk with a stranger who did not recognize him. Jefferson did not introduce himself, but the man talked freely about a number of things—including his extreme dislike for the president. Too late, the stranger discovered the identity of this plainly dressed horseman. Jefferson saved him from embarrassment, however, by assuring him that if the man in the White House were really as evil as his companion believed, he too would complain bitterly about him. On this particular outing, Jefferson won a new friend and supporter.

This same comfortable and relaxed manner was carried over into the president's home. For example, when a Pennsylvania farmer and his family visited the new capital, Jefferson invited them to the White House for dinner. There, elbow to elbow, these perfect strangers dined and discussed the cultivation of crops with the most famous farmer in America.

Unlike either Adams or Washington, Jefferson cared little for elegant formal receptions. In fact, during his administration the president of the United States gave no large official state dinners. Thomas Jefferson, however, often invited friends and neighbors in for quiet, informal suppers. Nearly every weekday evening a few members of Congress could be found around the White House table. At these little gatherings there were no stiff ceremonies. Upon arriving or departing the guests did not bow formally as they had done to previous presidents. Jefferson preferred a simple, democratic handshake. Usually he entertained in casual dress—once a foreign diplomat arrived to find him attired in house slippers and robe. When dinner was served, guests simply sat where they chose around a great oval table. At Jefferson's house, rank and titles were unimportant; even distinguished visiting dignitaries were not given privileged places. The food, prepared by the president's French chef, was excellent and abundant. Afterwards there were always homemade ice cream, good wine and pleasant conversation. Although the host was a poor public speaker, he was gifted and charming in quiet conversation. He could talk to anyone on almost any subject, and he always took special care to include even the shyest of his guests in the table talk.

Appropriately enough the White House itself was not in those days the elegant mansion it now is. It was huge, of course—big enough, Jefferson believed, for "two emperors, one pope and the grand lama." But throughout the eight years he lived there, it was only half finished. During the first two years the roof leaked, and the bedroom walls were unpainted. Inside there was little furniture and outside there were no rose gardens, shrubbery, or trees. The grounds, now so beautifully landscaped, were known then simply as Jefferson's "sheep pasture."

Nor was there anything very impressive about the City of Washington in the Territory of Columbia, as the new federal city was officially called. Jefferson took great pride in it. He picked its location and even helped plan its streets and parks. But construction of the capital city did not begin until the 1790s, and by 1801, when he became president, it was still a rustic little village of only 3,000 people. Unpaved Pennsylvania Avenue, which stretched from the White House a mile and a half through wilderness to the Capitol, was notable only for the stumps and wild alder bushes that blocked its way. When the weather was dry there were great clouds of dust; when it was wet there were vast pools of mud—and nearly always there were malaria-carrying mosquitoes. Even the Capitol was unfinished. Only its North Wing was ready for use by the United States Senate. Members of the House of Representatives had to use temporary quarters until the South Wing was completed ten years later. Yet, humble though its beginnings, Jefferson never doubted that Washington would someday be a splendid city to rival those of "the ancient republics of Greece and Rome."

The democratic simplicity of Jefferson's administration differed greatly from the more formal and aristocratic administrations of the Federalist presidents. Still, the differences were not as great as they seemed. The "Revolution of 1800" was much less "revolutionary" than either the Federalists feared or the Democratic-Republicans hoped. Thomas Jefferson was an intellectual, but he was also a very down-to-earth man. Before he became president he wrote learned essays in defense of the rights of states against the powers of the federal government. In the loftiest terms he denounced Hamilton and the Federalists for interpreting the Constitution too loosely. But once he became chief executive he used common sense, not noble theories, as his guide. He abandoned some, but not all, Federalist policies. To a far greater degree than most people recognized, his policies combined the best ideas from both political parties. He was, in short, a very flexible and practical politician as well as a brilliant and idealistic political thinker.

True to his Democratic-Republican principles, he tried to minimize the government's role in American life. He acted to eliminate government waste and cut government spending. He reduced the army and the navy to the barest essentials, and used the savings to pay a substantial portion of the national debt. The hated Alien and Sedition Acts expired during his administration and equally hated taxes

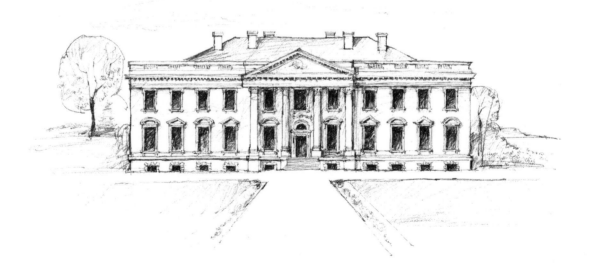

The White House of President Jefferson's day (above) was vastly different than the White House of today. The house was unfinished when Jefferson moved in on March 19, 1801, but this did not annoy the man who had spent many years remodeling Monticello. He began at once to improve the White House and give it style. For all Jefferson's simplicity of manners and his dedicated democracy, he liked beautiful surroundings —classical furniture, bright chintz and fashionable accessories.

were either repealed or reduced. Democratic-Republicans were appointed to every high office that became vacant, but there was no effort to change the sound and conservative financial policies established by Alexander Hamilton and the Federalists.

In matters of foreign policy, the president's actions were equally independent. When the Barbary pirates of North Africa, who had been attacking American trading vessels for years, demanded tribute money (bribes), he sent the navy into the Mediterranean Sea. Called the first Barbary War, this action brought new respect for the American flag and prestige to the United States navy.

When Great Britain went to war against Napoleonic France in 1803, Jefferson's aim was to keep the United States out of the fight. But both foreign powers interfered so openly with American rights to the use of the oceans that a policy of neutrality was not enough. So in 1807, the Congress, at Jefferson's urging, passed the Embargo Act to deny both Britain and France access to American markets and goods. This action, neither effective nor popular, did reflect a courageous president's determination to protect American rights, and seemed to be the only alternative to war or submission.

The American West was of special interest to the Virginia president. He had long envisioned a vast republic stretching from ocean to ocean. In time, he believed, there would be an American "empire of liberty" covering "the whole northern, if not the southern, continent" of the New World. He had no definite plans for acquiring this vast territory, nor did he have reason to believe that any of it would be obtained during his administration. But in 1803, to his own astonishment, France offered to sell the Louisiana Territory to the United States for the amazing price of three cents an acre. Thus, in a single stroke, the United States could double its size and win control of the Mississippi river. Although the Louisiana Purchase would be one of his greatest achievements, the president was a reluctant buyer. There was, of course, no specific Constitutional provision for the purchase of land from foreign countries—even at bargain rates. In so doing, he had to adopt Hamilton's theory of "loose construction" and, as he said, "stretch the Constitution till it cracked." Hamilton had little chance to gloat, however. In 1804 he was killed by Aaron Burr in a duel. The notorious Burr himself was tried for treason in 1806. He was acquitted, but it seems certain that he was guilty, nevertheless, of a "deep, dark, wicked, and widespread conspiracy" to separate western territory from the United States.

Immediately after the Louisiana Purchase Jefferson sent the explorers Meriweather Lewis and William Clark on their famous expedition to the headwaters of the Missouri and on to the Pacific Ocean. He also sent other adventurers, including Zebulon Pike, to explore and record the vast reaches of the Louisiana Territory.

Clearly, these years in Washington were among the busiest of his long and

active life. Still, he found time to take his goose-quill pen in hand to write his loved ones back in Albemarle County. Sealed with "Kisses" and "Tenderest love," these letters reveal the joy and pride he felt in his family. Always he asked for more letters in return. "Perhaps you think you have nothing to say to me," he once wrote Patsy. "It is a great deal to say [that] you are all well, or that one has a cold. . . . Besides that, there is not a sprig of grass that shoots uninteresting to me; nor any thing that moves, from yourself down to Bergere. . . . Write, then, dear daughter punctually."

To his dozen grandchildren he sent loving advice and poems and pictures for the scrapbooks he required them to keep. More often than they liked, he also inquired about their devotion to their studies. When he heard that one of them was progressing well, he was quick to offer grandfatherly praise. To "My Dear Ellen," his five-year-old granddaughter, he wrote soon after he became President: "I have received your letter and am very happy to learn you have made such rapid progress in learning. When I left Monticello you could not read and now I find you can not only read but write also." In closing he told her to be "a very good girl" and he gave the letter "20 kisses." In fact, as Jefferson knew, Ellen could neither read nor write at the age of five. Her letter was written by her mother, but her grandfather would not spoil the fun. When she did learn to write letters of her own, Ellen was usually a very regular correspondent. But one year, when she was nine, she fell behind, and according to her grandfather, owed him four letters. It was a bill, he teased, that must "be soon paid off [or] I shall send the sheriff after you." In the same letter,

OVERLEAF: *Burning of the Philadelphia*
Jefferson, determined to stop the Barbary pirates, dispatched ships in 1801 to the Mediterranean to blockade Tripoli. Naval hero Stephen Decatur sailed a small ship up to the captured *U.S.S. Philadelphia* in the harbor, set her afire, and then sailed away with only one casualty.
COURTESY MARINERS MUSEUM

he asked her, if she did not have the mumps, to put on her "boots & spurs & ride to Monticello" to report on how his garden grew. By return mail, the embarrassed granddaughter admitted that she had started many letters, but finished none. "But now I am determined to do it, . . . to show you I have not forgotten you."

Occasionally, when he too failed to write often enough, his grandchildren wrote scolding letters of their own. From his twelve-year-old grandson he received a brief note:

> Dear Grandpa:
>
> I wish to see you very much I am sorry that you wont write to me. This leter will make twice I have wrote to you and if you dont answer this leter I shant write to you any more.
>
> your most affectionate
> Grand Son Francis Eppes

Apparently the president responded, for the lad wrote his grandfather a great many more letters.

Ellen's older sister Anne also sent him her complaints: "This is the fourth letter I have written to my Dear Grand Papa without receiving an answer." When he did write, he sent her seeds and instructions for keeping his garden. Like her famous grandfather, Anne knew and loved every flower, plant, shrub and tree at Monticello.

From time to time, the grandchildren put aside their letters and with their parents took the four-day journey to Washington to see the president firsthand. On one of these trips, Patsy made history by having the first baby ever born in the White House. Appropriately enough, the baby was named after his grandfather's good friend, James Madison, the father of the Constitution.

The day came, of course, when their grandfather's stay in the White House was over. In March, 1809, Jefferson's second term of office expired. His party would have been more than happy to renominate him for a third term. But the Virginia statesman refused. Eight years had been enough for Washington and eight were enough for him. "Never did a prisoner, released from his chains, feel such relief as I shall on shaking off the shackles of power." As he had hoped, Madison was elected to put on those "shackles."

On his last day in office, Jefferson declined Madison's invitation to ride in his carriage to the inauguration. All of the inaugural honors, he said, belonged to his successor. Jefferson left the presidency as modestly as he had entered it. Almost unnoticed he rode up Pennsylvania Avenue, hitched Wildair in front of the Capitol, and joined the audience to watch the fourth president of the United States take the oath of office. "This day I return to the people and my proper seat is among them."

Patriarch on the Mountaintop

In 1809 the retired third president of the United States returned to his beloved Monticello. The worries and frustrations of high office were beginning to tell on him. His tall frame was not as ramrod straight as it once was. His loose-jointed stride was less spirited. Exhausted by forty years of concern for the nation's welfare, he was grateful to come home at last.

During a lifetime of public service Jefferson had found little time for his personal affairs. Yet, despite his prolonged absences, he had managed to keep up with the planting, cultivation and harvesting of his crops. For years, he often boasted, his vegetable garden near the kitchen produced the first peas in all of Albemarle County. He had even supervised the landscaping of the mansion's spacious grounds. But until he left the White House there was never time enough for such simple delights as flowers. Now, in his old age, the planter-statesman turned with great enthusiasm to the cultivation of tulips, hyacinths, irises and marigolds.

As he readily admitted, he could hardly tell one bulb from another at first. His granddaughter, Anne Randolph, for many years the resident chief gardener, was now married and could offer advice only by letter. "What is to become of our flowers?" he wrote soon after his return. "I left them so entirely to yourself, that I never knew anything about them, what they are, where they grow, what is to be done for them. You must really make out a book of instructions." Anne knew that

Thomas Jefferson
The president was very fond of this
1800 life portrait by Rembrandt Peale,
and it was popular for engravings.
COURTESY WHITE HOUSE HISTORICAL ASSOCIATION

Monticello (below) at Charlottesville,
Virginia. Jefferson planned every detail of
the mansion he had built on his mountaintop,
even making most materials on the
place. This is the view shown on the reverse
side of the Jefferson nickel. Right, another view
of Monticello and the pond where fish
caught in nearby rivers and streams were kept
alive and fresh until needed for the table. Water
for freshening the fishpond was supplied from cisterns
which held rainwater from the walkways and roofs.
COURTESY VIRGINIA STATE TRAVEL SERVICE

her grandfather was not as helpless as he pretended. But she sent her instructions just the same.

With Anne's assistance and some ideas of his own, the amateur gardener laid out a winding garden walk and a number of large oval beds on the west lawn. Soon, the mountain was ablaze with flowers.

Jefferson now found ample opportunity to reflect upon the changes that time had brought to Monticello. He remembered how majestic the mountain looked from Shadwell, his boyhood home in the valley below. He remembered, too, that spring day so long before when he first canoed across the swollen waters of the Rivanna to roam the wilds of its green and sunny slopes. Then the mountain looked much as it had when Peter Jefferson first set eyes on it in the 1730s. It was still a beautifully wild and untamed height from which to view the great Blue Ridge. The hardwood forests in the valley were smaller and the clearings greater. The wolves, so plentiful when Jefferson's father first came to this remote wilderness, had retreated before the advance of civilization. Now there were settlers and the villages of Charlottesville and Milton.

In 1767 Jefferson had given the mountain its name and planted cherry trees there. The next year he had its highest point leveled, and in 1769 a cellar was dug in the stiff red clay of the summit. Then for a dozen years the construction continued. Originally he hoped to have it finished before he married. But in 1772, his expectations of an early completion abandoned, he brought his bride to the humble cottage they called Honeymoon Lodge.

As these memories came rushing back, the old gentleman felt joy, not sadness. Martha lived with him only ten years. But they were the best years of his long life. He remembered her beauty, her gentle disposition, and most of all her music. He could still almost see and hear her, frail and small, singing in a soft clear voice, as she sat at the handsome English piano he imported for her wedding gift. The years had passed so rapidly that it seemed like only yesterday when they moved their belongings out of the cottage into the sparkling new mansion. It was, he remembered, one of the happiest moments of their life together—and one of their last. Soon after Monticello was finished, she was buried beside three of their children under the great oak in the little cemetery.

Gazing toward the mansion across the flower beds on the west lawn, Jefferson wondered what Martha would think of his splendid home now. In the 1790s much of the original structure was torn down. Perhaps with her gone the old Monticello recalled too much of the past. Perhaps, too, his taste had matured and the original design no longer satisfied his sense of beauty. Whatever the reason, he called back the carpenters to build a new Monticello on the mountaintop. To those bold enough to inquire why, he replied only that "architecture is my delight, and putting up, and

52

pulling down, one of my favorite amusements."

Indeed, as long as he could remember, buildings fascinated him. He was critical of most public and private buildings of colonial America. He thought the great homes of Virginia tasteless and too elaborate. As he said, New World architecture was "ugly, uncomfortable, and happily perishable." To satisfy his longing for more pleasing structures he designed many buildings in his lifetime. In Albemarle County alone, government offices, country homes, a church, and even a jail were constructed from his plans. He also designed the Capitol building in Richmond and the Rotunda and pavilions of the University of Virginia. But Monticello was his favorite project and his most important contribution to American architecture.

The new mansion required ten years to complete. Larger and even more beautiful than the original, it fitted snugly on the mountain top. It was elegant yet simple, a model of grace and dignity in a wilderness setting. To visitors then and now the new Monticello with its graceful white-domed center roof, its plain classical columns and its native red brick exterior was a breathtaking sight. To a famous French duke who saw it during Jefferson's lifetime, it was not only the finest house in all America, but one to rival "the most pleasant mansions of France and England."

Unfortunately, the retired statesman's private fortune was in less satisfactory condition. Although he lived elegantly and owned more than 10,000 acres and

nearly 200 slaves, he was always short of cash. During Martha's lifetime he enjoyed considerable prosperity. But as the years passed and the demands of public life increased, he found it necessary to neglect his personal affairs. Unable either to continue his law practice or attend personally to his farms, he watched his financial condition slowly deteriorate. Nor was he ever adequately paid by the government. His expenses were usually greater than his salary. In truth, his tastes were richer than he was, and he nearly always lived beyond his means. When he retired from the White House in 1809, he was astonished to learn that he was fully $25,000 in debt. Although he lived another seventeen years he never overcame his financial difficulties. When he died his estate was sold to pay his long overdue bills.

In large measure, Jefferson's money worries were shared by many Virginia planters. Once the richest colony, the Old Dominion became in the early 1800s one of the nation's poorest states. Economically it was falling behind the industrial states of the North and its worn-out soils could not compete with the new agricultural states of the West. In his mind, Virginia was the "Eden of the United States." But in fact neither its land nor its climate were as ideal for farming as he believed. Endless cycles of tobacco and corn exhausted the soil. Severe winters, late frosts and dry autumns reduced the harvests. Occasional downpours "unknown since Noah's flood" washed away the crops, and the burning sun parched and cracked the brick-red surface of his fields.

Three long-neglected farms at Monticello, Elk Hill, and Poplar Forest required Jefferson's full attention. Once his flower beds were established, he put aside his memories of the past and turned to the day-to-day routine of agriculture. He took an interest in every detail of farming. Crop rotation, sheep raising, the uses of manure, the planting of clover and potatoes all caught his attention. Farm machinery fascinated him, and his farms were always equipped with the latest in labor-saving equipment. If word came of a new threshing machine, or a new device for planting grain he had to have it. Whatever the implement he usually owned it, and almost always he found ways to improve its operation, often redesigning these machines entirely. Occasionally, as in the case of his famous "moldboard plow," he invented them himself.

A very practical man, who was always short of money, Jefferson tried to make Monticello as self-sufficient as possible. Instead of buying household needs from distant American or European cities, he tried to have them manufactured at home. His blacksmith shop made tools, utensils, cutlery and almost every other item of hardware needed on the mountain. Each year his family and servants used 2,000 yards of linen, cotton and woolen cloth, much of it carded, spun and woven in his shops on the mountain. The bricks and lumber needed to build and rebuild Monticello were made in Jefferson's own kiln and sawmill. The flour and cornmeal used in his kitchen were produced in his grist mill. Even the nails his carpenters used were produced in the little "naillery" located on Mulberry Row on the southern slope below the mansion. As with most of the other goods produced in his shops, the surplus nails were traded or sold to buy beef, butter, coffee, tea, sugar, rice, brandy and other necessities for Monticello's table.

Jefferson took a special interest in the work and the workers in his shops. When the naillery was started he was there, toiling and sweating beside a dozen young slave boys until they mastered the operation. He saw to it that black children were given light chores, and slaves of every age knew that he would reward their best efforts with praise and cash bonuses. Each morning after breakfast he went from shop to shop, pausing to offer encouragement here, inquiring about a worker's health there, promising to improve conditions somewhere else. Occasionally problems arose, as when Isaac, the burly black foreman of the naillery, caught a worker stealing a large quantity of nails. Brought weeping and begging into the master's study, the thief was let off with only a quiet scolding. To Isaac's amazement the man became one of his most loyal and energetic hands. Even a slave, Jefferson believed, could be led more easily than he could be driven. Gentle words were often more persuasive than a whip.

Although he owned many slaves, Jefferson hated slavery. In the Declaration of Independence he wrote that "all men are created equal." In his *Notes on Virginia* he vigorously condemned a labor system that permitted one man to own another. Repeatedly during his public career he attempted to end the hated institution. To his great satisfaction, the international sale of slaves was eventually forbidden. But his plan for the gradual emancipation or freeing of the slaves was never tried.

For practical and moral reasons, he did not even free his own Negroes. They were necessary for the operation of his farms, and he doubted their ability to survive as free men in a white world. Thus slavery was a necessary evil. He could not abandon it, but he could at least treat its victims as human beings.

In order to lighten the burden of his slaves, and perhaps to ease his own guilty conscience, Jefferson constantly searched for ways to decrease his need for them. Accordingly, Monticello was notable for clever inventions that provided ease and convenience for the master with a minimum of effort from the servant.

In the dining room, as Jefferson never tired of demonstrating, guests could enjoy a splendid meal without a servant in sight. Dumbwaiters, or portable stands loaded with food, could be conveniently located so that diners might serve themselves. Wine could be raised from the cellar on a miniature hand-operated elevator. Additional courses and table service could be placed on a revolving buffet in the hall and swiveled silently into the dining room. Later, in the quiet of his study, the host and an overnight guest could enjoy midnight refreshments without troubling

the kitchen staff. At the push of a button little doors on a handsome wooden box would fly open to reveal a bottle of wine and a plate of light cakes.

These and other useful contrivances made Monticello a showcase for the inventive mind of its master. Visitors in his day, as in ours, marveled at the amazing variety of his inventions. There was an indoor weathervane and a music stand that could be used by four musicians at once. Over the east entrance a massive seven-day clock with faces both indoors and out told the hours of the day and the days of the week. And to provide him comfort while he wrote his many letters, there was an ingenious red-leather swivel chaise lounge and revolving writing table.

Closely related to Jefferson's lifelong fascination with practical gadgets and inventions was his interest in science and technology. America, he often observed, was "a country where there is more to do than men to do it." Wherever he traveled he searched for new ways to make machines do man's work. In France he became interested in flying or "aerial navigation" by means of gas-filled balloons. In Holland he studied wheelbarrows and wind-driven sawmills, and in England steam-powered engines caught his eye. In almost every case he tried to improve the operation of these inventions and apply them to American needs. Although he never did so, he planned to invent a small and inexpensive machine to "wash the linen, knead the bread, beat the hominy, churn the butter, turn the spit, and do all other household offices which require only a regular mechanical motion."

Scientific theories also interested him. But even here he had practical goals in mind. Most of his scientific investigations were conducted to disprove false notions about America. European misconceptions about his native land offended his sense of truth and patriotism. He was especially outraged by the assertions of the famous French scientist Buffon, who speculated that the American climate was harmful to both man and beast. European animals, Buffon argued, were not only larger and more numerous but superior to American animals in every way.

To prove otherwise, Jefferson sent the Frenchman the bones, hide, and antlers of American moose, deer, elk and caribou. With his customary attention to details, he collected information on the weight and size of various American and European animals. Comparing his findings, he informed Buffon that the American cow weighed more than its European cousin, and the American otter weighed 2.3 pounds more than the European otter. For final proof of the superiority of New World animal life, he assembled the skeleton of a mammoth. He was incorrect in his belief that this hairy, long-tusked beast still roamed the forests of North America. But even Buffon had to agree that it was one of "the largest terrestrial beings."

The scientific-minded Virginian also quarreled with Europeans who argued that human life in the New World was less vigorous and intelligent than in Europe. The United States, he admitted, had not yet produced a poet of the stature of Homer nor a thinker the equal of Voltaire. But despite its youth and its tiny population, it could already claim such "hopeful proofs of genius" as a Franklin in science, a Washington in war, and a Rittenhouse in astronomy. Had he been less modest, he might have added a Jefferson in statecraft.

In like manner Jefferson defended the American Indian against Buffon's charges that the Indian, too, was made weak and stupid by the New World climate. The red man, Jefferson declared, was uncommonly brave and strong. He

The kitchen at Monticello where all meals were prepared for the Jefferson family and hordes of visitors. It was common for Jefferson to have several dozen people at meals, and for days or weeks at a time. All bread had to be baked here and a fine steer would be consumed in one day. The kitchen is below ground and connected to the dining room by tunnels and stairs.

COURTESY THOMAS JEFFERSON MEMORIAL FOUNDATION

Above, Jefferson's bed which was in an alcove between his study and his bedroom. At right is his swivel chair and swivel table at which he wrote much of his voluminous correspondence. The long leg rest added to his comfort during long hours of work and reading. Left, a view of the library at Monticello.

was trustworthy, affectionate, and "fully equal to a white man." In some cases, he argued, the first inhabitants of America were so eloquent of speech that even such ancient orators as Demosthenes and Cicero compared unfavorably.

Jefferson consistently pursued his study of American natural history. During his years as secretary of state, his New York apartment served as an experiment station for rice plants. When he left Monticello to become vice president, his baggage contained a collection of ancient bones belonging to an extinct creature, twelve feet long and six feet high, he called the "great-claw or megalonyx." Later, during his presidency, an unfinished room of the White House was cluttered with the remains of ancient giants of the American past. For many years he studied Indian dialects in the hope of proving that the red man was among the earth's oldest and noblest peoples. Unfortunately, his invaluable collection of tribal vocabularies was lost to pirates when his possessions were shipped back to Virginia in 1809.

Narrow-minded Europeans were reluctant to admit the virtues of the American climate and the nobility of its animal and human life. But they quickly recognized that in Jefferson the New World had produced a man of immense learning and wide interests. In addition to English, he could read Greek, Latin, French, Italian and Spanish. His personal library was the largest in all America. He was a noted scientist and inventor, a distinguished statesman, a gentleman farmer, and an honored diplomat. In his own lifetime he was recognized at home and abroad as a symbol of human intelligence and creativity.

But those who knew him well saw his more human characteristics. Always a private person, he jealously guarded his personal and family life from public view. Admirers from afar could respect his accomplishments, but only in the company of intimate friends and loved ones did he reveal his true self. To Alexander Hamilton he was a brilliant political enemy; to Count Buffon he was a learned student of American natural history; to the people of the United States he was the eloquent champion of democracy. To his many grandchildren he was the kindly, soft-spoken, affectionate and good-humored old gentleman they called Grand Papa.

During his presidential years Jefferson's younger daughter Polly died. Her passing at the age of twenty-five, he wrote a friend, robbed him of "half of all I have." Fortunately, Patsy, the remaining half, lived a long and fruitful life. Her eleven children and Polly's one lived most of each year at Monticello. They worshipped him with that special devotion that children reserve only for grandfathers. To them he was "cheerfulness, love, wisdom." As one of the Randolph children remembered: "I cannot describe the feelings of admiration, and love that existed in my heart towards him. I looked upon him as being too great and good for my comprehension; and yet I felt no fear to approach him."

On sunny afternoons when the old patriarch strolled in his gardens, the grand-children always "raced after and before him." In season, one recalled "he would gather fruit for us, seek out the ripest figs, or bring down the cherries from on high above our heads with a long stick, at the end of which there was a hook and little net bag."

At other times he took charge of their games. "One of our earliest amuse-ments," a granddaughter wrote long after his death, "was in running races on the terrace, or around the lawn. He placed us according to our ages, giving the young-est and smallest the start of all the others by some yards . . . and then he raised his arm high, with his white handkerchief in his hand . . . and slowly counted three, at which number he dropped the handkerchief, and we started off." All received rewards of dried fruit for the effort: "three figs, prunes or dates to the victor, two to the second, and one to the laggers who came in last."

In addition to the lively company of his grandchildren, the retired president had a steady stream of visitors. Gracious hospitality was a way of life in early Virginia and Jefferson was among Virginia's most gracious hosts. "We had per-sons from abroad, from all the States of the Union, from every part of the State, men, women, and children," one of the grandchildren later marveled. "Almost every day . . . brought . . . people of wealth, fashion, men in office, professional men, military and civil, lawyers, doctors, Protestant clergymen, Catholic priests, mem-bers of Congress, foreign ministers, missionaries, Indian agents, tourists, travellers, artists." Some were invited, some were not. Some were strangers, others were friends. But in this day of few public accommodations, none was denied bed and board at Monticello.

Patsy, who played hostess to this great throng, occasionally found places to put up as many as fifty overnight guests. The overseer, who lacked Patsy's unfail-ing good humor, grumbled that at the height of the "visitor season" "a fine beef" lasted only "a day or two." Overnight, the guests' horses could eat so much of a wagonload of hay that "the next morning there would not be enough left to make a hen's nest."

Amid such confusion Jefferson could neither work nor relax. He enjoyed the evenings of lively conversation that this interesting variety of humanity could pro-vide. Yet he found it necessary to escape periodically to Poplar Forest some nine-ty miles and two days away. The visitors at Monticello continued, in the over-seer's words, to "eat him out of house and home." But at least in this lovely eight-sided second home he could find refuge.

Poplar Forest brought no release from his burdensome correspondence, however. One of history's most tireless pen men, he wrote perhaps as many as

Right, aerial view of Thomas Jefferson's "academical village," the heart of the University of Virginia which he founded and helped to build. Above, the north facade of the rotunda, with the Ezekiel Liberty Bell statue of Jefferson. Left, the famed serpentine walls, only one brick in thickness, and gently curving for strength. Jefferson, who supervised all construction details, personally taught the bricklayers how to build these walls.
COURTESY VIRGINIA STATE TRAVEL SERVICE

50,000 letters in his lifetime. Although retired, he found that his advice was still much in demand. Even late in his seventies he received as many as 1,200 letters in a single year. Determined to answer them all he frequently complained that "from sunrise to one or two o'clock, and often from dinner to dark, I am drudging at the writing-table."

Of course all of it was not drudgery. Some of it, especially his correspondence with John Adams, was immensely satisfying. The two friends of the Revolutionary period drifted apart during Adam's presidency. But when Polly died in 1804, Adams's vivacious wife Abigail broke the silence with a letter of sympathy to her husband's old friend. At that point Jefferson tried to renew the relationship. But the gruff old New Englander refused. Later, however, after Jefferson's retirement, Adams changed his mind. "I always loved Jefferson," he told a mutual friend, "and still love him." Overjoyed with this news, the Virginian shouted "this is enough for me." In 1812 the two former presidents put aside the unpleasant political memories of the past and began anew the famous Adams-Jefferson correspondence.

As the circle of the Founding Fathers grew smaller and their many aging friends from the revolutionary era passed away, they grew closer. For fourteen years the letters flowed between Massachusetts and Virginia in an uninterrupted stream until death claimed both Jefferson and Adams within a few hours of the same day.

The reconciliation with Adams was one of the most satisfying accomplishments of Jefferson's old age. The other was the founding of the University of Virginia. Since his days in the House of Delegates he had believed that the future of democratic government depended on public education. Throughout his life he agitated for a system of state-supported general education. His dreams for public elementary and secondary schools were never fully realized. But in 1817, the university he wanted was chartered.

He designed its first buildings, and supervised every detail of their construction. Although in his late seventies when the project began, his towering figure could be seen daily at the building site in nearby Charlottesville, calling instructions, reading plans, making decisions. When there were not enough skilled workers, he gave on-the-job training to bricklayers and carpenters. When a craftsman proved clumsy with his tools, those wrinkled but steady hands showed him how to proceed. During bad weather, when his rheumatism made the ride down the mountain too painful, he watched the work progress with his telescope from the mountaintop.

The University was his "holy cause." He even planned the curriculum, hired the faculty, and selected the library books. When at last its doors opened in 1825, it pleased him as much as Monticello and the Declaration of Independence.

The founding of the University of Virginia was the last and proudest of Jefferson's many triumphs. The year after its opening his health failed rapidly. In March, 1826, convinced of his approaching death, the eighty-three-year-old patriarch made out his will. Although his long, thin body was racked with pain and disease, he held desperately to life until the early days of July. His doctor kept a record of the old stateman's last hours: "Until the 2nd [and] 3rd of July, he spoke freely of his approaching death; made all his arrangements with his grandson, Mr. Randolph, in regard to his private affairs. . . . In the course of the day and night of the 2nd of July, he was affected with stupor, with intervals of wakefulness and consciousness." In the evening of the third he inquired, " 'Oh Doctor, are you still there?' in a voice, however, that was husky and indistinct. He then asked, 'Is it the Fourth?' to which I replied, 'It soon will be.' These were the last words I heard him utter."

The end came at ten minutes before one o'clock in the afternoon of July 4, 1826, the fiftieth anniversary of the Declaration of Independence. The next day, in a soft summer rain, the philosopher of freedom was laid to rest beside Martha and Polly, beneath the great oak. There were no formal speeches, no funeral parades, no official state ceremonies. There were only the private mourning of his family and the quiet of his mountain.

The nation's third president
wished his monument to be a
plain obelisk with "the following
inscription, and not a word more."

Here was buried
Thomas Jefferson
Author of the Declaration
of American Independence
of the Statute of Virginia for
religious freedom & Father of the
University of Virginia

A Heritage for Free Men

On July 4, 1826, the nation's fiftieth birthday, John Adams also lay dying. His last words, "Thomas Jefferson still survives," were uttered three hours after the Virginian's death. But Adams was right just the same. Thomas Jefferson still survives in the noblest ideals of the United States. The democratic principles that make this a great nation were the principles he set forth in 1776:

> We hold these truths to be self-evident, that all men are created equal, that they are endowed by their Creator with certain unalienable Rights, that among these are Life, Liberty, and the pursuit of Happiness. That to secure these rights, Governments are instituted among Men, deriving their just powers from the consent of the governed. . . .

That one paragraph is the heart and soul of Jefferson's philosophy of freedom. In it one finds his belief that the Creator gave all men and women the same rights and liberties, including the freedom of thought and action necessary for their full happiness as human beings. Jefferson did not mean, of course, that all people are equally strong and intelligent, or even that all are equally wise and good. But he did believe that God intended for all of His children to have the same opportunities to exercise the freedoms He gave them. Moreover, because governments exist only for the protection of these God-given rights, Jefferson believed that the best governments were those ruled by the people themselves. However many the mistakes of popular self-government, they would be few when compared to those of hereditary rulers. Kings and aristocrats, he knew, were exceedingly poor protectors of human happiness.

It is our good fortune that after two centuries the stirring words of Jefferson's Declaration of Independence remain as vital and valid as the day he wrote them. Because in life he gave those words meaning, he left in death a priceless heritage for free men.

Index

us, in times of peace, standing Armies without the Consent of our legislatures." —— He has
with others to subject us to a jurisdiction foreign to our constitution, and unacknowledged by o
armed troops among us: — For protecting them, by a mock Trial, from Punishment for an
our Trade with all parts of the world: — For imposing Taxes on us without our Consent:
Seas to be tried for pretended offences: —— For abolishing the free System of English Laws in
so as to render it at once an example and fit instrument for introducing the same absolute ru
altering fundamentally the Forms of our Governments: —— For suspending our own Legist
He has abdicated Government here, by declaring us out of his Protection and waging War ag
of our People. —— He is at this time transporting large Armies of foreign Mercenaries to comple
scarcely paralleled in the most barbarous ages, and totally unworthy the Head of a civilized nation
their Country, to become the executioners of their friends and Brethren, or to fall themselves by their
inhabitants of our frontiers, the merciless Indian Savages, whose known rule of warfare, is an undis
have Petitioned for Redress in the most humble terms: Our repeated Petitions have been answered o
is unfit to be the ruler of a free People. Nor have We been wanting in attentions to our Brittish
able jurisdiction over us. We have reminded them of the circumstances of our emigration and set
by the ties of our common kindred to disavow these usurpations, which, would inevitably inte
consanguinity. We must, therefore, acquiesce in the necessity, which denounces our Separate

We, therefore, the Representatives of the united States of America, in g
tentions, do, in the Name, and by Authority of the good People of these Colonies, solemnly publis
States; that they are Absolved from all Allegiance to the British Crown, and that all politica
that as Free and Independent States, they have full Power to levy War, conclude Peace, cor
States may of right do. —— And for the support of this Declaration, with a firm re
and our sacred Honor.

Button Gwinnett
Lyman Hall
Geo Walton.

Wm Hooper
Joseph Hewes,
John Penn

Edward Rutledge.

Thos Heyward Junr.
Thomas Lynch Junr.
Arthur Middleton

Saml C
Wm Paca
Thos Stone
Charles Carroll

George
Richard

Th Jeff

Benj Fra
Thos Nelson
Francis light
Carter Bra